RED DEMON

HIDEKI NODA

RED DEMON

OBERON BOOKS
LONDON

WWW.OBERONBOOKS.COM

First published in 2003 by Oberon Books Ltd
521 Caledonian Road, London N7 9RH
Tel: +44 (0) 20 7607 3637 / Fax: +44 (0) 20 7607 3629
e-mail: info@oberonbooks.com
www.oberonbooks.com

A catalogue record for this book is available from the British
Library.

PB ISBN: 9781840023572

Visit www.oberonbooks.com to read more about all our books
and to buy them. You will also find features, author interviews and
news of any author events, and you can sign up for e-newsletters
so that you're always first to hear about our new releases.

Noda Map and Amy Kassai Ltd present *Red Demon*, first performance was at the Young Vic, London on 31 January 2003 with the following cast:

MIZUKANE	Simon Gregor
THAT WOMAN	Tamzin Griffin
TOMBI	Marcello Magni
VILLAGER	Samantha McDonald
VILLAGER	Clive Mendus
RED DEMON	Hideki Noda
VILLAGER	Ofo Uhiara
VILLAGER	Matt Wilkinson
Director	Hideki Noda
Set and Costume Co-Designers	Miriam Buether and
	Vicki Mortimer
Lighting Designer	Rick Fisher
Music Supervisor	Yukio Takatsu
Sound Designer	Sarah Weltman
Production Manager	Paul Russell
Deputy Stage Manager	Clare Loxley
Assistant Stage Manager	Kayo Furuta
Costume Supervisor	Hattie Barsby
Set Construction	Mark Wiltshire
	(Set Up Scenery)
Scenic Artist	Richard Nutbourne

Characters

THAT WOMAN
an outcast, lives by the beach

TOMBI
her brother, a moron

MIZUKANE
a chancer, infatuated with That Woman

VILLAGERS
insiders, working folk

RED DEMON
outsider, perceived as a monster

The action takes place within a small, closed island community. The stage setting should be very simple. The one object of note is a wardrobe by which, in various guises, much of the story is enacted.

Note

For this production, as indicated in the text, Japanese was the language used by Red Demon. For other productions, the native language of the actor playing Red Demon should be employed.

PROLOGUE

A wardrobe stands alone on stage.

A man (RED DEMON) enters.

He stands before the wardrobe, then opens it.

Sound of ocean waves.

Other players begin to enter, in time to the rhythm of the waves.

Sound reaches climax.

The man steps through the doors of the wardrobe, just before it is picked up and hurled about.

Sound of a fierce storm.

SCENE 1

Beach. The storm rages. Three figures are washed up. VILLAGERS enter and find them lying on the sand.

MAN ONE: They're still breathing.

MAN TWO: Pull 'em up quick.

MAN ONE: We gotta keep 'em warm.

WOMAN ONE: Any more of 'em?

WOMAN TWO: Doesn't look like it.

MAN ONE: Christ…it's *them…*

MAN TWO: They made it back…

WOMAN TWO: Look! That Woman's here too!

MAN ONE: That Woman?

WOMAN ONE: Sling her back in the sea. She's not bleedin' worth it.

MAN TWO: What are you talking about? She's *alive.*

WOMAN TWO: Just leave her where she is will you!

HAG's shack. HAG brings THAT WOMAN a bowl of soup.

THAT WOMAN: Thank you. It tastes so good.

HAG: That's shark's fin soup. Special. We thought we'd lost you to the waterfall at the end of the sea.

THAT WOMAN: What was that?

HAG: Aye. Thought you'd sailed right off the edge of the ocean and –

THAT WOMAN: No, I mean the soup. What did you say it was?

HAG: Oh, shark's fin. The fin of the shark…

THAT WOMAN: This isn't what shark's fin tastes like.

HAG: What, you've had it before, have you?

THAT WOMAN: Of course I have. Every day out at sea.

Cliff. As TOMBI talks, THAT WOMAN climbs to the top and hurls herself off.

TOMBI: *(To audience.)* My little sister died two days after eating that shark's fin soup. After she had so narrowly escaped from the jaws of death, she went and threw herself off a cliff, right back into the sea.

MAN ONE: And after all the trouble we went to to save her in the first place.

WOMAN ONE: A spiteful little tart till the end, no two ways about it.

MAN TWO: Smashed to bits on the rocks, doesn't make sense…

WOMAN TWO: Don't look at me. That's just the kind of That Woman that she was.

TOMBI: *(To audience.)* No-one can fathom the reason my little sister died. Except me. I've got an idea why. I mean, I may be as thick as two planks, oh not that I myself think I'm thick as two planks but everybody and his dog always says that I am thick as two planks, if not three planks, so sometimes I start thinking that I might be and that's why I don't feel like telling you why my little sister really died because you'll just be furious with me if I tell you, that's why.

MAN ONE: We won't be furious.

TOMBI: No, I know it from long experience.

WOMAN TWO: Come on, tell us. We won't be angry with you.

TOMBI: Cross your heart?

WOMAN TWO: *(Crossing her heart.)* And hope to die.

TOMBI: My little sister died because she ate that shark's fin soup.

WOMAN TWO: Oh pack it up!

MAN TWO: What d'you take us for?

WOMAN ONE: You saying she was poisoned by the very soup we slaved to make for her?

MAN ONE: He comes out with it doesn't he? Shame you didn't take the plunge along with her Tombi!

TOMBI: *(To audience.)* See, I knew they'd be furious with me. I should have kept my mouth shut like I wanted to. When people like me who have something missing upstairs tell stories, the stories always have something missing too. That's why you have to bear with me and hear me out, okay? I'll tell you as best I can. 'The Story of My Little Sister who was Killed by Eating a Bowl of Shark's Fin Soup.' Okay? It begins on a day like the day she lost her life, on a beach in the evening, a beach swept clean by a fierce storm…

Beach. TOMBI and VILLAGERS comb the sand for valuables.

MAN THREE: I've had it. Now there.

TOMBI: Not for me.

MAN FOUR: How many bottles you picked up Tombi?

TOMBI: One, two, a whole lot.

MAN FOUR: Three comes after two, not a whole lot.

MAN THREE: Just a load of empties, look.

TOMBI: But I really got a whole lot.

MAN FOUR: That's what I asked: How many?

TOMBI: One, two, a whole lot.

MAN FIVE: Bloody useless. All you get's the roar of a storm when you put 'em up to your ear.

WOMAN THREE: We took in some good gear after last year's storms though, didn't we?

MAN FIVE: Eh?

WOMAN THREE: Mahoganny sea chest. Fetched a pretty penny.

MAN FIVE: So?

WOMAN THREE: That silver-plated compass.

MAN FIVE: Sea was kind to us.

They all stop for a moment and stare out. Sound of ocean waves. Behind them, RED DEMON draws himself up from the sand. They slowly turn. They freeze at the sight of him. They flee.

MAN THREE: Get me a drink and make it a double.

MAN FOUR: You look like you've seen a ghost.

MAN THREE: I saw it. It was of another world…

MAN FOUR: What was?

MAN THREE: A monster…it's not human I tell you…

MAN FOUR: A monster?

MAN THREE: I'm telling you, with my own two eyes.

MAN FOUR: Go on.

MAN THREE: It was like right large with a face covered in fuzz and it was soaked to the bone and it had water blisters…

MAN FOUR: What d'you say?

MAN THREE: Water blisters.

MAN FOUR: Right large you say, with a fuzzy face, soaked to the bone and…*water blisters?*

MAN THREE: Water blisters!

MAN FOUR: What the hell IS IT?

MAN THREE: I DON'T KNOW!

MEN: What? / What? / What?

MAN FOUR: Beats me 'n all. Though I do admit, it is incredible.

WOMAN THREE: Incredible? In what way?

MAN FOUR: Just plain incredible. Everyone's talking about it.

WOMAN THREE: Have you seen it then?

MAN FOUR: What? Yes!

WOMAN THREE: You haven't actually seen it, have you.

MAN FOUR: 'Course I have! Front row seat, I had.

WOMAN THREE: So what kind of a monster was it?

MAN FOUR: All right then. It's face was a bright red, and not only its face. When it opened its gob you could see what looked like burning lava inside. And the minute it set its sights on me, it went 'snappety-crack', started charging like a bull at a bull fight. Behind me you've got the sheer drop of the cliff. And coming at me, head on, the beast, horns down…

WOMAN THREE: You mean it had horns?

MAN FOUR: Yeah-eh. And not only horns, it had *water blisters.*

WOMAN THREE: Water blisters?

MAN FOUR: Water blisters.

WOMAN THREE: You mean it's got horns, goes snappety-crack *and* it's got water blisters? What the bloody hell IS IT?!

MAN FOUR: I DON'T KNOW!

WOMEN THREE / FOUR / FIVE: *(Together.)* Did you hear that?

WOMAN THREE: My husband didn't just hear it, he saw it!

WOMAN FOUR: Yeah, well, so did mine.

WOMAN FIVE: So what. My husband got bitten by it.

WOMAN THREE: Lucky he wasn't eaten alive.

WOMAN FOUR: The monster eats humans.

WOMAN THREE: And other things besides.

WOMAN FIVE: What do you mean 'other things'?

WOMAN THREE: That calf that got eaten up last year?

WOMAN FOUR: What? You told me the Royal Goddess Princess Di ate that when she came down as a ghost.

WOMAN THREE: Ah, that was me talking bollocks. You wouldn't expect a goddess to do a thing like that would you?

WOMAN FIVE: Nah. Besides, only half that calf was eaten. The other half's still alive and kicking around somewhere.

WOMAN FOUR: That's it! The monster's come back to finish it off.

WOMAN FIVE: God, what is it?!

WOMAN THREE: It's got horns and water blisters and it goes snappety-crack before it takes a chunk out of you.

WOMAN FOUR: Snappety-crack? What's that?

WOMAN THREE: Demon language for 'twist your head off'.

WOMAN FIVE: What? *(They freeze.)* What did you just say?

WOMAN FOUR: She just said 'demon', didn't she? She did!

WOMAN THREE: Yeah, so, it's a demon. With a red face.

WOMAN FIVE: But what's a red demon doing here?!

WOMAN THREE: It's got to be because of you-know-who.

WOMAN FOUR: You-know-who…?

WOMAN THREE: You know. That Woman.

WOMAN FIVE: *(Slowly.)* It's That Woman who's behind all this…

WOMAN FOUR: She summoned the red demon here…

ALL: That… *Woman…*

SCENE 2

THAT WOMAN's house. THAT WOMAN is gutting fish. TOMBI rushes in, starts manically closing windows and shutters.

THAT WOMAN: Hey, leave those windows alone! You trying to give me heat-stroke or something? *(TOMBI collapses in the corner.)* What's up? What're you shivering like that for, you got a fever?

TOMBI: You really don't know?

THAT WOMAN: Oh, Tombi…

TOMBI: What?

THAT WOMAN: Are you worried about a red demon coming here, is that it?

TOMBI: So you did know!

THAT WOMAN: Well, the word is everyone's saying I sent for it.

TOMBI: Yeah, that's right. Did you Sis?

THAT WOMAN: Did I what?

TOMBI: Did you send…for a red demon?

THAT WOMAN: You're as bad as them.

TOMBI: You've been known to send for some weird and wacky things in your time.

THAT WOMAN: Oh really? Such as?

TOMBI: Well. These storms, you know. King Kong, yes. And the Love Goddess Britney, when she appeared on the beach. That was your doing too, people say.

THAT WOMAN: They'll blame me for any old shite.

TOMBI: Must be because you're so gorgeous, I reckon.

THAT WOMAN: Do you have any idea what that means?

TOMBI: Yes I do. 'Gorgeous' means a woman who a man wants to pounce on.

THAT WOMAN: You think that up all by yourself?

TOMBI: Well, I heard it from Mizukane. He said that all women fall into two categories: the ones you want to pounce on and the ones you've *got* to pounce on.

THAT WOMAN: Not a vast range.

TOMBI: Mm, yes.

THAT WOMAN: When it comes to men, there's only one category: Evil sods who like to shag quick and move on quicker. It's at least easy to remember.

TOMBI: You've got an attitude problem, you know that? All Mizukane wants to do is get on your good side.

THAT WOMAN: All he wants is to get on top of me, that's what he wants. He doesn't even know my name.

TOMBI: Not so. He's always asking me about my little sister.

THAT WOMAN: 'Little Sister' isn't a name Tombi.

TOMBI: Yes. No.

THAT WOMAN: Anyway, I couldn't give a toss what I'm called or what anyone thinks. So.

TOMBI sees RED DEMON over his sister's shoulder.

TOMBI: Ahhh!

THAT WOMAN: What's the matter now?

TOMBI: I just remembered something quite important.

THAT WOMAN: Yeah, what?

TOMBI: I saw a red demon.

THAT WOMAN: When?

TOMBI: On the beach…the bottles…I was picking one up…I…maybe we shouldn't get too relaxed…I mean…it's behind you.

THAT WOMAN: Very good, Tombi. You know, you and your ideas are getting that little bit more bonkers every day.

Trembling with fear, TOMBI goes around his sister to change places with her. It's about the most ingenious method of showing her RED DEMON he can come up with. By then, however, RED DEMON is gone.

TOMBI: I tell you it was there! Right behind you!

THAT WOMAN: Look. Nothing shocks me anymore, okay? Not snakes behind me, not demons behind me, nothing. Nothing but people. What people do never ceases to amaze.

TOMBI: *(To audience.)* I was really taken by what my little sister said that day. But when she came face to face with the Red Demon the day after that, she might have felt like eating those words.

SCENE 3

Boat. THAT WOMAN steps in. RED DEMON approaches under water, like a shark. He leaps in. THAT WOMAN screams, then freezes.

THAT WOMAN: *(Delirious with fear.)* They say it's an old wives' tale that when you come upon a bear, you should play dead. 'Crap', I remember my mother saying. 'You've got to look a bear straight in the eye…then start creeping… slowly backwards…telling it softly all the time… "I'm not going to hurt you." ' *(She inches backwards, but hits the side of the boat.)* Shit. Should've asked her what you do when you're on a boat.

RED DEMON: @@@@@@@. [Water.]

THAT WOMAN: Listen, I don't taste any good. Horrendous, to be quite frank.

RED DEMON: @@@@@@@@@@@@@@@@@@@@@. [I've been out at sea for ages and have had nothing to drink. Give me some water please.]

RED DEMON attempts to explain himself through gestures, but they remain unclear, even to the audience. For instance, he does not gesture 'to drink water' with his hand, but rather by getting on his back on the floor and sticking out his tongue. We have no way of comprehending his gestures or the kind of life he leads.

THAT WOMAN: You can't eat humans. We're eighty per cent water.

RED DEMON: @@@@@@@@@@@@@@@.

THAT WOMAN: No, I'm water! Water!

RED DEMON lies on the floor and sticks out his tongue, nodding towards THAT WOMAN's water bottle at her waist.

Wait…you want water?

RED DEMON: @@@@@@@@. [I want water.]

THAT WOMAN: In that case, what I just told you…not strictly true. Actually, between you and me, humans aren't made of water at all. No. We're made of blood and and and and thick, rancid meat. Totally unchewable. Eurgh.

RED DEMON: @@@@@. [Water!]

THAT WOMAN: Absolutely.

She quickly thrusts the bottle down in front of RED DEMON.

RED DEMON: *(Still on his back.)* @@@@@@@@. [No, you feed it to me.]

THAT WOMAN: What? What do you want?

RED DEMON: @@@@@@@@@@@@@@@@@@@@. [What kind of country is this anyway where they don't know even know how to give someone a drink?]

THAT WOMAN: Huh? Oh, you can't use your hands when you drink, eh? Okay. Just…don't eat me.

She gives RED DEMON water. RED DEMON calms down a bit, as does THAT WOMAN. Suddenly RED DEMON leaps up again; she leaps back.

RED DEMON: @@@@@. [Thank you.]

THAT WOMAN: All right, easy…now what?…what usually comes after a little drink?…if it was me, let's see…I s'pose I'd be looking for a spot of lunch.

RED DEMON licks his chops. This is a gesture of affection to RED DEMON.

This is ridiculous, this can't be real, can't be happening, it's, this is, this is – All right! Look. If I've got to be eaten, I wouldn't mind saying a couple of words first. My life has not exactly been a total breeze. You wouldn't wanna write home about it. But I've survived. I've come through. And now, and now, and now, now this! *(Looks dead at him.)* You really must be a demon. You're a demon because you eat humans.

RED DEMON opens his arms to her.

Blackout.

SCENE 4

THAT WOMAN's house. TOMBI and MIZUKANE enter. THAT WOMAN works repairing a net, apparently oblivious to what has transpired earlier. MIZUKANE sidles up to her.

MIZUKANE: Listen…can I just say…*vis à vis*… *(Gestures 'me' and 'you'.)* …there's no one who cares about you like me. Isn't that right, Tombi?

TOMBI: Huh?

MIZUKANE: Go on, do your stuff, lad.

TOMBI: Hey, how goes it Sis? Now, just grit your teeth… and let Mizukane slip it in.

MIZUKANE: What you doing?

TOMBI: What, what? Don't you want to give her one?

MIZUKANE: *(To THAT WOMAN.)* What I want is for you to open up a little bit, that's all.

TOMBI: Her mind or her legs?

MIZUKANE: Oih smartarse. *(To THAT WOMAN.)* I'm on your side. You know what they call you, don't you?

TOMBI: That Woman.

MIZUKANE: Correct. That Woman. Anything with the prefix 'That': not good news. That Wife. That Shop. *(To audience.)* That play. *(To THAT WOMAN.)* But as for you… That…stunning…wondrous…Woman… *(Mouths 'Piss off' to TOMBI. He smiles charmingly at THAT WOMAN, as TOMBI gets the hint.)*

THAT WOMAN: Where're you going Tombi?

TOMBI: He told me to disappear when he started going on about 'That'.

MIZUKANE: Eh? No. All I said was check out the beach for bottles. Perfect now, tide's out.

TOMBI: Sure. You told me to get lots and lots of them all night, so many that I wouldn't come back.

MIZUKANE: Yes and why did I say that?

TOMBI: Because so you could stay and try to get into my sister's –

MIZUKANE: Because I am the only mug on this island generous enough to take them off your hands. Give you a decent price. Help you out.

TOMBI: Yes.

MIZUKANE: As a mate.

TOMBI: Thank you, mate.

THAT WOMAN: Yeah and you've probably got some ulterior motive for that too.

MIZUKANE: What is this, Nuremburg? Listen, I'm a new man. I'm nothing like *them*. This lot bash dolphins to death for a coupla quid after a storm. They wouldn't recognise real treasure if it washed up on their laps. I mean you know what's in those bottles, don't you Tombi?

TOMBI: I do.

MIZUKANE: That…which is beyond the sea…

THAT WOMAN: Good grief. He's a poet.

MIZUKANE: What you find beyond the sea is no dream of a mere poet. It *exists*. And this coastline is the closest thing we've got to it. And the fishermen here…catch fish. Wankers. I fish for what's inside the bottles. You have to treat each and every one with respect. Take a peek.

TOMBI: *(Looking in a bottle.)* Ah, it's there all right.

MIZUKANE: Here.

TOMBI: What does it say?

MIZUKANE: *(Looking.)* Ha. Another poxy SOS.

TOMBI: That's all I ever get. I suppose people beyond the sea are really in trouble a lot of the time.

MIZUKANE: You wait. The time will come when what's inside this bottle will fetch more than all the fish in the sea.

Sound of a loud rattling noise from an old wardrobe.

What's that?

THAT WOMAN: What?

MIZUKANE: That. *(They listen.)* Your face. You look like you've just seen a demon.

THAT WOMAN: Huh. 'Demon.' You jest.

TOMBI: It's true, you know. I was the one who met the demon. Not once, but twice.

MIZUKANE: Tombi, there's no such thing.

TOMBI: Is too.

MIZUKANE: The demon's just a rumour spread around the beach.

TOMBI: You wouldn't be talking like that if you saw it.

MIZUKANE: I'd be talking like that *especially* if I saw it. I'd waltz straight up to it, shake its hand. Plant a big wet one right on its mouth. My door. Is open. To all.

RED DEMON bursts out of the wardrobe.

RED DEMON: RRRRrrrrrrggghhh!!!

MIZUKANE: *(Jumping a mile.)* Whoooooah, what the fuck is that!!!

TOMBI: Looks demony to me…

MIZUKANE: Get me a hatchet, quick!

THAT WOMAN: What's your problem?

MIZUKANE: Keep your distance! Jesus Christ! How long's it been here?

THAT WOMAN: Since lunchtime. I gave him some water.

MIZUKANE: You're joking!

RED DEMON: @@@@@@@@@@@. [I'm starving to death.]

RED DEMON's gesture for 'hungry' looks like sniffing cocaine.

TOMBI: Gosh, the demon spoke.

MIZUKANE: Demons don't speak, donkey, they growl.

RED DEMON: @@@@@@@@@@@@@@@@@@@@@. [I'm not asking for much, just food and water please. And a bit of shut-eye. I'll do whatever you like once I'm back on my feet. I'm begging you. Isn't there one human being who understands what I'm saying?]

Beat.

TOMBI: That's one heck of a long growl.

THAT WOMAN: I think he's trying to tell us something.

RED DEMON: @@@@@@@@@@. [Okay. Just some food then, that's all.]

THAT WOMAN: I think he's trying to say he's hungry.

MIZUKANE: You call that a gesture for being hungry?!

THAT WOMAN: Yeah. Look. This is thirsty. *(She imitates the gesture for thirsty.)*

MIZUKANE: That?

THAT WOMAN: Yeah.

THAT WOMAN gives some water to RED DEMON, who drinks it in the same way as before.

See? He must be hungry now.

MIZUKANE: Tombi, listen up.

TOMBI: I'm all ears.

MIZUKANE: Go up to it and see if it eats you.

TOMBI: Me?

MIZUKANE: Don't you trust me, mate?

TOMBI: I do, mate.

MIZUKANE: Then get your arse over there.

TOMBI: Right.

TOMBI goes and stands before RED DEMON.

It's not eating me. Look. I can wiggle my bum and everything and it's not even touching it!

MIZUKANE: Must be full.

THAT WOMAN: Maybe he doesn't eat people.

MIZUKANE: Doesn't eat people? Doesn't eat – it's a demon for fuck's sake! A demon couldn't show its face in public if it didn't eat people! A minute from now, it'll be hungry all over again, it'll be back on the offensive. Watch.

THAT WOMAN: I thought you were going to go up and shake hands with him. Give him a big sloppy kiss.

MIZUKANE: Are you having a laugh?

TOMBI: *I'd* shake its hand.

MIZUKANE: What?

They watch as TOMBI calmy walks up to RED DEMON and proudly holds out his hand. This gesture however is interpreted by RED DEMON as a belligerent one.

RED DEMON: @@@@@@@@@@. [Get that hand away from me. Withdraw your hand!]

MIZUKANE: Christ, watch it!

THAT WOMAN: He won't do anything if we don't.

MIZUKANE: Oh yeah? One bite from this fella, you're history.

THAT WOMAN: That's what I thought, too. When he hugged me.

MIZUKANE: …hugged you…?

THAT WOMAN: Uh-huh.

MIZUKANE: I'm sorry, did you say…*hugged* you?

THAT WOMAN: He just squeezed me really tight.

MIZUKANE: And?

THAT WOMAN: Nothing.

MIZUKANE: Nothing? Do me a favour! A bloke's not gonna stop at a hug.

TOMBI: A bloke? Who says it's a bloke? It looks sort of blokey because it's a demon, but you never know…it could be just as well a woman.

THAT WOMAN: Never.

TOMBI: Why not?

THAT WOMAN: I can tell by the way he looks at me.

RED DEMON: @@@@@@@@. [Can't you see, I'm s-t-a-r-v-i-n-g.]

RED DEMON gives each of them in turn the same look.

THAT WOMAN: Yeah.

MIZUKANE: Tombi, now's our chance, throw the net!

TOMBI: *(Dropping net on the floor.)* Urgh.

THAT WOMAN: No, no, he's just asking for food.

TOMBI: Why don't we feed it then?

THAT WOMAN: He's turned down everything I can offer. Won't touch fish or rats or socks – actually the socks went down alright –

MIZUKANE: It eats humans!

THAT WOMAN: *(Ignoring MIZUKANE, to RED DEMON.)* What do you want? You're just trying to tell us you want to eat, aren't you?

RED DEMON: @@@@@@@. [You follow me?]

THAT WOMAN: I follow.

TOMBI: She's getting through to it!

MIZUKANE: Mind yourself. Could be asking whether or not it can put you top of the menu.

RED DEMON: @@@@@@@@? [Am I getting through to you?]

TOMBI: *(Simultaneously.)* Can…I…please…eat you?

THAT WOMAN: Sure.

The following action / dialogue is in slow-motion.

RED DEMON approaches them.

MIZUKANE: Don't give in! You're gonna get M-U-N-C-H-E-D…!!!

RED DEMON puts his arms around THAT WOMAN. TOMBI holds flowers over her shoulder. RED DEMON jumps on TOMBI, snatching the flowers from him and eating them hungrily…everything back to real time.

What was that?

TOMBI: Just some flowers.

THAT WOMAN: So that's what it eats. Flowers!

MIZUKANE: How d'you come up with that?

TOMBI: A hunch.

THAT WOMAN: Nice one Tombi! Quick, go and get some more, right now.

MIZUKANE: Wait. *(They all stop.)* Why are you doing all this…for a demon?

THAT WOMAN: All what?

MIZUKANE: What's going on here?

THAT WOMAN: Nothing.

They stare at each other.

MIZUKANE: Tombi. Go and tell the people on the beach, tell them a demon is about to gobble up your sister.

THAT WOMAN: No! Just go and get some flowers, okay?

MIZUKANE: She's gonna be eaten alive Tombi!

THAT WOMAN: Flowers, Tombi!

MIZUKANE: Your poor lovely sister Tombi!

TOMBI: Right.

MIZUKANE: Right? Which of us is right?

TOMBI: *(To audience.)* After that, I ran up and down the beach at twilight grabbing all the flowers I could and yelling 'My sister's going to get gobbled up!'

He runs about, grabbing flowers and yelling 'My sister's going to get gobbled up!'

SCENE 5

Wood. Trees transform into two VILLAGERS.

MAN: The Red Demon's here!

WOMAN: What? Where?

MAN: That Woman's house!

WOMAN: That Woman's house? Thank Christ for that.

MAN: Yeah but every time it eats someone it gets bigger and bigger! It's bloody massive!

WOMAN: Then we've got to kill it.

MAN: Aye but it'll be murder at night. I say we do it before the sun goes down.

TOMBI: *(To audience.)* The big problem was that while they were contemplating the best way to kill the Red Demon, the sun did in fact go down.

A WOMAN with baby appears. She bumps into RED DEMON. She puts down the baby in terror and flees. The baby starts crying. RED DEMON looks at it, then picks it up to pacify it. He rushes off with it. Trees transform into MOTHER and FATHER.

FATHER: Harold's been kidnapped!

MOTHER: Somebody, help us!

FATHER: It's your fault you daft bitch. You let him out of your sight.

MOTHER: I'm sorry, darling.

FATHER: You're not fit to be a mother, goddammit!

MOTHER: I know, I know. I'm rubbish. He was just having a quiet nap in the garden when this kidnapper jumped out and yelled 'Hand over the little tyke!'

FATHER: Everybody listen! Don't let your babies out of the house! The sound of crying babies. Everyone gathers round.

HEAD ELDER: Why have babies been brought to such a crucial meeting? Somebody SHUT THEM UP!

FATHER: Please, sir. We leave our babies at home, they'll be attacked by the Red Demon. We're desperate, sir.

MOTHER: It's all because of That Woman. Harold was eaten instead of her.

HEAD ELDER: Now hold on, we don't know for certain whether he has or he hasn't been.

VILLAGER: Are you mad? Their baby's all alone with that thing. What you saying? Little Harold's gonna eat the demon?

HEAD ELDER: Well no, not exactly…

MOTHER: So what are you saying?

HEAD ELDER: Why don't we just drop this question of who's going to eat who…

VILLAGER: Because that's all a beast thinks about. Morning, noon and night. Why d'you think it's called a beast?

FATHER: My mother-in-law's like that. Food on the brain twenty-four seven.

HEAD ELDER: A baby brought up by a wolf turns into a wolf, they say. Not that I've known many wolves in my day…

FATHER: Oh fantastic. So a baby brought up by a red demon is gonna –

MOTHER: We've got to get to Harold!

TOMBI enters.

HEAD ELDER: What do you think you're doing here Tombi?

VILLAGER. Tombi! Get your sister over here right now!

TOMBI: The Red Demon won't eat any baby, I don't think.

FATHER: What did he say?

TOMBI: The Red Demon doesn't eat humans. It eats flowers.

FATHER: Eh? Flowers?!

TOMBI: I saw it.

FATHER: You're dead from the neck up, you know that pal.

HEAD ELDER: Wait a mo. I've had a thought. If this Red Demon does eat flowers, as Tombi here says, then perhaps…yes…we could lure it to a sea cave. Use flowers from the beach as bait and drive it in.

Beat.

MOTHER: Sweetie-pie?

FATHER: Fuck knows.

MOTHER: Tombi's definitely as thick as two toilet seats, but it might just work.

HEAD ELDER: Right everyone. Let's see those flowers.

Flowers are scattered. RED DEMON enters, holding baby. VILLAGERS observe him from afar.

FATHER: Look…it's eating them…

HEAD ELDER: That's a demon all right.

VILLAGER: Ssshhh…it's turning this way…

MOTHER: It's got Harold! He's alive!

FATHER: And it's trying to feed him a daffodil.

HEAD ELDER: It must think humans eat flowers too.

MOTHER: Harold's just eaten it! And he's smiling!

FATHER: This is torture. My little boy already turning into a demon.

HEAD ELDER: He does look a bit redder, come to think of it.

MOTHER: We've got to hurry, please!

HEAD ELDER: Well quite. It's off guard…consuming daffs by the lorry-load…

VILLAGER: So let's get it!

After much effort, they finally trap RED DEMON in a cave.

HEAD ELDER: Excellent work everyone. Jolly well done.

FATHER: Put the champagne on ice. Harold's still stuck in there.

HEAD ELDER: At least it's not going to escape. Of that we can be certain.

MOTHER: Oh Harold…

HEAD ELDER: Hush now. The demon eats *flowers*, my dear.

MOTHER: Just because it eats flowers doesn't mean it won't eat my baby up too!

HEAD ELDER: Oh I'm quite sure that it won't –

MOTHER: We like vegetables, but we still eat meat, don't we?

HEAD ELDER: Yes, well, be that as it may…

He turns and the scene shifts to MIZUKANE's house. Everyone transforms into ELDERS.

…Mizukane, we elders have come here because we understand you have knowledge of things beyond the sea.

MIZUKANE: What a touch.

HEAD ELDER: Mm?

MIZUKANE: Doorstepping a bloke who can't be bothered to catch a single fish. I like your style.

ELDER ONE: Has the Red Demon come here from beyond the sea?

MIZUKANE: I dunno. Shouldn't you boys have the answer to that one?

ELDER TWO: Wisdom about life does not extend to life beyond the sea.

MIZUKANE: So you admit there is a 'beyond', eh? I was under the impression that ships just sailed on and on, then…plopped off the edge.

ELDER THREE: That is what I still hold to be true.

MIZUKANE: Really. Well you wanna know what's beyond the sea? Same thing that's in the bottles. Nothing.

HEAD ELDER: The demon. You know about the Red Demon.

MIZUKANE: You catch fish in a net. You gather information in a net. Isn't that why it's called 'the net'?

ELDER ONE: Rescue the baby.

MIZUKANE: Now you're asking something.

HEAD ELDER: I shan't put up with this a moment longer. Youngsters who turn on fancy retorts whever they feel like it.

MIZUKANE: 'Turn on'? I'm not a tap, grandad.

HEAD ELDER: What did you say to me?!

MIZUKANE: *(Christ, I need this.)* Sir. When asking a favour from somebody, it is customary to bow one's head.

HEAD ELDER: What?

MIZUKANE: Bow…one's…head.

HEAD ELDER: Never.

MIZUKANE: Fine.

ELDER TWO: Sir, I think we ought to act like palms…and bend with the wind.

The ELDERS reluctantly bow their heads.

MIZUKANE: Well well well. Three holes in the road.

SCENE 6

Ouside THAT WOMAN's house. MIZUKANE and TOMBI follow THAT WOMAN as she goes about her chores.

MIZUKANE: Call it a weakness, call it a crime, but I've never been able to refuse a man who's bowed down in front of me. *(THAT WOMAN snorts.)* Tell you what though people. We ought to strike now, while the iron's hot.

THAT WOMAN: So why don't you go and talk to him?

MIZUKANE: Eh?

THAT WOMAN: Yeah. See if the demon falls for all that drivel about the bottles.

MIZUKANE: There wasn't any info on red demons in the bottles.

THAT WOMAN: Poor you.

MIZUKANE: Oh come on. You're the one with the special connection. Have a word and get the baby back. I'm telling you, you'll be hailed The Heroine of the Beach.

THAT WOMAN: And who'll be the hero, you?

MIZUKANE: Not at all.

TOMBI: What am I?

MIZUKANE: You're the nitwit brother of the heroine.

TOMBI: 'Nitwit brother'. Hm. Has a nice ring to it.

THAT WOMAN: You can shove it. They see me communicating with a red demon, they're going to think I'm one too.

MIZUKANE: *(Exasperated.)* Your turn, mate.

TOMBI: You shouldn't lose heart, Sis.

THAT WOMAN: The trouble with you darling brother, is *you've* lost your marbles.

TOMBI: Maybe. But I've never lost my sense of hope.

THAT WOMAN: Oh you're mistaken. We're pretty hopeless, the two of us.

TOMBI: Mm. Not me.

THAT WOMAN: You are.

TOMBI: I'm not.

THAT WOMAN: Are.

TOMBI: Aren't.

THAT WOMAN: ARE!…Every generation of this family has found the same. People hate people who come from the outside. It's all the reason they need.

MIZUKANE: But this lot will *accept* you now. Don't you see?

THAT WOMAN: Thanks but no thanks.

MIZUKANE: Don't you even feel sorry for little Harry?

THAT WOMAN: Nope.

MIZUKANE: Then you really must have no heart at all.

TOMBI: Hang on, I thought that the women without any hearts turned you on Mizukane. You said they were your kind of ladies.

MIZUKANE: Not now Tombi.

TOMBI: That you really get a proper stonker when you saw them.

MIZUKANE: Tombi! *(To THAT WOMAN.)* Listen, I'm just thinking of you, okay? I've been willing the day to come when you could be accepted, when there'd be no more secrets and nothing to hide. That day is here.

THAT WOMAN: And that's why you run for hatchets every time you see a demon?

MIZUKANE: It's a monster.

THAT WOMAN: Sure. And once the baby's rescued, you're all planning on beating that monster to death, aren't you?

MIZUKANE: Never in a blue moon.

THAT WOMAN: Liar.

They stare at each other.

Make a deal with the villagers. After the Red Demon hands over little Harold, you promise not to go near him for three – no make it seven, whole days. Agreed?

Scene shifts to Villagers' meeting, as HEAD ELDER stands up.

HEAD ELDER: Agreed.

MIZUKANE: Huh?

HEAD ELDER: We can live with that. Seven days, the Red Demon shall not be touched. But in exchange, we demand that That Woman rescues the baby from the sea cave immediately. Tell her that, Mizukane.

TOMBI: *(Audience.)* I wonder what was going through my sister's mind on her way to the cave. She never uttered the word 'hopeless' after that. I still can't fathom the meaning of that word. I've never encountered anything hopeless before. Please, somebody, where can I find something hopeless?

SCENE 7

Entrance to sea cave. THAT WOMAN approaches RED DEMON.

RED DEMON: Mama.

THAT WOMAN: Huh?

RED DEMON: Mama.

THAT WOMAN: You looking for your mama?

RED DEMON: Mama.

THAT WOMAN: You do speak a language.

RED DEMON: @@@@@@@@@@. [Mama is you.]

THAT WOMAN: If you think you're gonna get through like that, forget it. This is for your benefit. The first thing you've got to do is learn our language. Me…teach…you…

language. I sound like bloody Tarzan. Tombi, could you come here for a moment please?

TOMBI: *(To RED DEMON.)* Uh, hi.

THAT WOMAN: You, demon. Him, moron. So, friends.

TOMBI: I am its friend?

THAT WOMAN: Shut up will you. *(To RED DEMON.)* My name…is Fu-ku.

TOMBI: What that's your name?!!

THAT WOMAN: *(To RED DEMON.)* What's yours?

No response.

Fuku. Me, Fuku.

TOMBI: Bloody heck.

RED DEMON: Fu-ku. Fuck you.

THAT WOMAN: Fuck me? Well it's progress. *(Indicating each of them.)* Mama, fuck. Moron, Tombi. Demon. Now you.

RED DEMON: Fuck Tombi…

THAT WOMAN: If he can just say his own name it'll prove he's human.

TOMBI: *(Still shell-shocked.)* Fuku?

THAT WOMAN glares at him.

RED DEMON: Hideki.

THAT WOMAN: *(Whirling round.)* What'd you say?

RED DEMON: @@@@@@@@. [My name. It's Hideki.]

THAT WOMAN: Hideki.

RED DEMON: Hideki. Fuck. Moron.

They communicate with each other for a while using only their names. Finally RED DEMON uses his own name.

TOMBI: Wow-wee. Feels like we've known each other for years.

THAT WOMAN: Hideki, give back the baby. Baby. Tombi, act like a baby.

TOMBI: Huh?

THAT WOMAN: A baby.

TOMBI: Oh.

TOMBI does a very poor impression of a baby.

MIZUKANE: *(Arriving.)* Hopeless. Check this out.

He does a very skillful impression.

RED DEMON: Ohh, Akanbo.

TOMBI: He got it!

MIZUKANE starts making notes.

THAT WOMAN: What are you doing?

MIZUKANE: Keeping tabs, sweetheart, re. your friend. *(Continues writing.)* …real name…Hideki… 'Baby' … equals…'Akanbo'…

THAT WOMAN: Hideki, give Akanbo back to Mama Fuck. *(To TOMBI.)* Do 'giving back'.

TOMBI: 'Giving back?' That's a toughie…

MIZUKANE and TOMBI do impressions, at first failing, then succeeding.

RED DEMON: Kaesu??

THAT WOMAN: Kaesu? Okay. Kaesu akanbo to Mama Fuck.

RED DEMON gets the baby from the cave and hands it to THAT WOMAN.

TOMBI: Yes!!

Entrance to sea cave. VILLAGERS surround it. FATHER and MOTHER snatch up the baby from THAT WOMAN.

MOTHER: Harold!

FATHER: Now burn the Red Demon!

THAT WOMAN: Wait, wait…

VILLAGER: Light the torches!

THAT WOMAN: But your promise!

MOTHER: You any idea what I've been through?!

FATHER: Don't waste your breath, love.

MOTHER: No 'course you don't. How could *you* understand a mother's pain!

THAT WOMAN: But the Head Elder –

HEAD ELDER: If you're gonna stand between us and the Red Demon, we'll just have to burn the both of you.

THAT WOMAN: Yes but the Head Elder – You've promised.

HEAD ELDER: D'you think we're gonna let that thing loose again and risk any more of our children?

THAT WOMAN: He's not a *thing*, he's a human being!

VILLAGER: Hear that? 'Not a thing!'

FATHER: For all we know, she's one of them!

THAT WOMAN: All right, okay. You want to set fire to this cave, go ahead. But remember, with that fire you'll be showing your sins to the whole world. The more wicked the sin, the higher the flames will climb. So come on. I'm watching. Let's see just how wicked you can be.

MOTHER: It's you who's going to hell.

FATHER / HEAD ELDER / VILLAGER: *(Together.)* Burn the cave!

TOMBI: *(To audience.)* Then the villagers armed themselves to the hilt, lit burning torches and forced their way into the cave. How many miracles can we expect in life? It's beyond me. But this one time, I can say for certain that a miracle did happen. The people who held torches in their hands froze where they stood, holding their breath, with their eyes wide open.

Inside the cave.

MIZUKANE: Tombi…

TOMBI: Yes?

MIZUKANE: Look…

TOMBI looks about and gasps. They stare incredulously for a long moment.

We're inside the bottle…

TOMBI: They're so beautiful…

THAT WOMAN: Hideki. Did you paint these pictures on the walls?

RED DEMON speaks in the native language of the actor.

RED DEMON: This is the place that I come from. These trees, that only I know, these golden birds, that only I know, the lapis lazuli butterflies, the scarlet fruits, the crystal streams and the coconuts that were imprinted on my memory before I drifted to this shore. And this is a song from my faraway homeland.

He sings, in the actors' native language. He finishes his song and turns to them.

THAT WOMAN: *(Slowly.)* Gods have always come from beyond the sea.

TOMBI: *(To audience.)* This put a terrible fear into the villagers. They had never dreamt that someone they called 'That Woman' might have the powers to invoke the presence of a god. They fled the cave in awe. And so one miracle had run its course. But another was in the post. It arrived three days later and it was quite a prize beauty.

Outside THAT WOMAN's house.

THAT WOMAN: I can't get him to do it at all.

MIZUKANE: Do what?

THAT WOMAN: I feel like I'd be better off sticking my head in a blender. We've got to get him to speak.

MIZUKANE: It's just your gesturing. Leave it to the professionals.

TOMBI: Yeah. The professionals.

MIZUKANE: So, what's on your mind?

THAT WOMAN: I want to teach him, 'Now is the winter of our discontent.' *(MIZUKANE hesitates.)* Well go on then.

MIZUKANE: I wouldn't recommend that straight off.

THAT WOMAN: No?

MIZUKANE: Not really.

THAT WOMAN: Okay. How about this one: 'He who leaves the *pièce de résistance* is always the politest one.'

Beat.

TOMBI: Even I don't get that one.

RED DEMON: @@@@@@@@@.

THAT WOMAN: Precisely.

RED DEMON: @@@@@@@@@@@.

THAT WOMAN: What? Ooh, you cheeky sod!

RED DEMON: @@@@@@@.

THAT WOMAN laughs.

MIZUKANE: Is this what they call bi-lingual?

TOMBI: In just three days too! Ask Red Demon if this is how everyone speaks in his country.

THAT WOMAN: @@@@@@@.

RED DEMON: @@.

THAT WOMAN: Yep.

MIZUKANE: So @ is 'yes'.

RED DEMON: @@@@@@@@. [Please stop calling me Red Demon.]

THAT WOMAN: @@@@. [Sorry.]

TOMBI: What'd he say?

THAT WOMAN: He wants us to stop referring to him as Red Demon.

MIZUKANE: Listen what country does he come from? That's the real teaser isn't it?

THAT WOMAN: @@@@@@.

RED DEMON: Red Monde.

TOMBI: Red Monde?

MIZUKANE: Red Monde? That's just 'Red Demon' with a little twist.

TOMBI: Hm, oh yeah.

MIZUKANE: Look, are the paintings in the cave pictures of its home, of the land beyond the sea, or what?

THAT WOMAN: I don't know if I can do that. *(To RED DEMON.)* Sea? Sea? You understand 'sea'? *(She gestures uselessly.)* Shit.

RED DEMON: @@ ...Umi.

TOMBI: Sea is 'Umi!'

THAT WOMAN: Yeah, but 'beyond' is going to be impossible. *(Gesturing.)* Here. Beyond. Here. Beyond.

MIZUKANE: It's beyond me.

TOMBI: I think Red Demon's beyond help.

THAT WOMAN: No! Everyone needs something beyond themselves. Why d'you think we climb mountains? Can't you see? If I can climb up, over words... I might actually be able to look out at last...to beyond the sea...

TOMBI: *(To audience.)* Mizukane used to make up stories about that place from time to time, but now I heard my own little sister talk, I thought to myself they might be true after all. Everybody needs to imagine a place beyond them that they could go to.

THAT WOMAN: Tombi, we've spent our whole lives living with the energy of the dead. The whole story of our family belongs to the bottom of the sea, clinging for dear life to nothing but grudges. I see our mother, rowing out there to die. The white waves, rising in clouds to the heavens, like a pedestal for the setting sun. And the sun itself, staring out from that pedestal, like her own despair. And why? Hopelessness. Living with nothing in your heart and nothing to come.

TOMBI: Mmm. 'Energy of the dead.' I am such a moron. All I can think of when you say that is a zombie. My mother's despair and my sister's despair are definitely beyond me.

Huge sound of birds rising, wings beating. They all look out, long moment.

What's that?

MIZUKANE: Gannets offshore. There'll be a giant school of bluefish under that lot.

TOMBI: Wow!

MIZUKANE: Surefire sign of a big catch.

TOMBI: *(To audience.)* But it wasn't just a sign of a big catch. The flock of gannets would be a warning to us…of course at the time we didn't think that one bit…

RED DEMON: *(Delightedly.)* Oh Goto!

TOMBI: *(Delightedly, simultaneously.)* Oh God!

RED DEMON: Oh Goto!

TOMBI: Oh Goto!

MIZUKANE: Hey listen to that! 'Oh God' is 'Oh God' even in Red Demon language!

RED DEMON: Oh Goto!

MIZUKANE: *(Pointing at RED DEMON.)* Oh God!

RED DEMON: Oh God!

They all repeat the words delightedly, pointing at each other and the gannets.

MIZUKANE: I can't believe it!

THAT WOMAN: You're getting through!

TOMBI: He's getting through!

MIZUKANE: *(Deeply moved.)* I talked with the Red Demon. I actually talked with him. He understands what I say. We… conversed. And what's more…he's a bloody nice bloke too! Oh God!

TOMBI: *(To audience.)* And before we knew it, the second miracle had happened and there he was, Mizukane, telling everyone up and down the beach…

Beach. VILLAGERS jostle around MIZUKANE, TOMBI and RED DEMON.

MIZUKANE: Roll up, roll up, your very own red demon, yes your very own god. Let's see the smiley happy faces. Hello darling, how are we?

VILLAGER: It's amazing, it's just so like you know… amazing!

MIZUKANE: Amazing! Right from the horse's mouth! Yes indeed, clap your eyes, cop a feel, the demon does not disappoint!

VILLAGER ONE: What a lovely little demon, makes you wanna take it home doesn't it?

VILLAGER TWO: I know. Said some right nice things to me.

VILLAGER ONE: Saucy bugger! 'Ere, can I have another go?

MIZUKANE: Many as you like, my darling.

VILLAGER THREE: Eh up, how long we got to wait? I'm growing a beard stood here.

MIZUKANE: Growing a beard, sir, don't you worry. One word from the demon, watch the years drop off. Trust me.

VILLAGER FOUR: We've come from two beaches over!

MIZUKANE: Sir, madame, if you'd care to follow my assistant…

TOMBI shows them RED DEMON.

VILLAGER FIVE: Ooh, look at that….I feel faint!

VILLAGER FOUR: Come on love, next to it then…

She moves next to RED DEMON, as VILLAGER FOUR takes out a camera.

That's it, that's it…little more…nice and tight…Yee-ES!

THAT WOMAN enters. Everyone turns and stares.

Beat.

VILLAGER SIX: If you don't mind, we have reservations.

THAT WOMAN: *(Accusingly to MIZUKANE.)* Reservations?

MIZUKANE: Of course, sir.

VILLAGER SEVEN: When my nan was little, a mermaid landed on her beach. She ate some of its flesh and guess what? She's alive today. And my great grandma too. It's become a sort of family tradition.

TOMBI shows them RED DEMON.

Meaty.

VILLAGER SIX: I'll need a napkin, this could get messy. *(They both laugh.)*

RED DEMON: @@@@@@@@. [What are they on about?]

THAT WOMAN: Nothing. *(To VILLAGERS.)* Please, show him some respect.

VILLAGER SIX: I'll respect it all right. Get me a knife and fork. *(They laugh again.)*

RED DEMON: @@@@@@@@. [Tell me what they're saying!]

THAT WOMAN: You're disgusting…

RED DEMON: @@@@@@@@!!! [Bloody well tell me!]

THAT WOMAN: @@@@@@ [They want to eat demon meat.]

RED DEMON @@@@? [Oh they do do they?]

RED DEMON walks up to the VILLAGERS.

He extends his arm towards them.

@@@! [Eat and live!]

Beat.

VILLAGER SIX: What's it say?

THAT WOMAN: 'Eat and live.'

Beat.

VILLAGER SEVEN: Good thinking.

She bites RED DEMON on the arm, RED DEMON yells.

Not bad, actually. How do I look?

VILLAGER SIX: Years younger already, love. It's uncanny.

They leave.

TOMBI: Sis, Sis…ever since Red Demon showed us his good side, people have been very nice. Yes. Stopped giving the cold shoulders and everything.

THAT WOMAN: …

MIZUKANE: No, he's right, they've been brilliant.

THAT WOMAN: …

MIZUKANE: They have. They love us.

TOMBI: Sis…could you just say a big thank you to it. Could you? It would mean a whole lot, you know.

MIZUKANE: Definitely.

THAT WOMAN: You tell him yourself!

TOMBI: *(To audience.)* That day my sister was in quite a definite mood. But she know what was what. The villagers had come to accept Red Demon, yes. But not as a human Not ever as a human.

Beach. THAT WOMAN sits alone with RED DEMON.

THAT WOMAN: The tide is out. I wonder how many empty bottles lie waiting to be found tonight.

Silence.

Who was it who said that thing about the sea? You know... there it is...smashing against the coast...back and forth... days and months...years...but what ever does it want? It never tells.

She looks at RED DEMON.

I don't know what to say. I wish...I wish you could understand me. I need you to understand me, to talk...in my language...and I know you can't.

RED DEMON slowly reaches out, touches her gently. She looks up at him softly.

Is it really like the pictures? The land beyond the sea?

They gaze at each other.

Won't you tell me? Tell me. Please. Tell me.

RED DEMON: I have a dream.

THAT WOMAN: What?

RED DEMON: I have a dream...that one day this world will rise up and live out the true meaning of its creed: We hold these truths to be self-evident, that all men are created equal.

THAT WOMAN: I understood you a lot better when you spoke total gibberish, I mean, growling like a wild beast. But now, the more I can pick out snippets of what you say, the less sense you seem to be making.

RED DEMON: I have a dream.

THAT WOMAN: Hideki, I'm frightened that when I come to put together all the separate words you say, I won't have a clue as to what you mean by them.

RED DEMON takes her hand and swings her gently.

RED DEMON: Let freedom ring.

THAT WOMAN: Like what? Like Quasimodo at Notre Dame?

RED DEMON: Let freedom ring.

THAT WOMAN: This freedom thing should ring the bell, is that it? What for, though? I don't follow you. Who are you, anyway? Where do you come from? Why were you drifting the sea?

RED DEMON: I have a dream…that one day freedom will ring from every hill, from every mountainside, every village and every hamlet, from every state and every city… let freedom ring.

THAT WOMAN slowly takes RED DEMON's hand and swings him gently.

SCENE 11

Beach. MIZUKANE and TOMBI enter.

MIZUKANE: So here's the gig. There are women, and they do exist old pal, whose rationale for life relies entirely on playing the innocent. I kid thee not. These damsels constitute, in effect, the 'What, who me?' school of crumpet.

TOMBI: Mmm. Crumpets.

MIZUKANE: All that fluttering of hearts, hands to the face, palpitations? Bollocks. These Birds Mean Business.

TOMBI: They do?

MIZUKANE: Crap in your cornflakes, nail your cock to the carpet. Soon as you turn your back.

TOMBI: To the…your… *(He winces.)*

MIZUKANE: I've seen it. I've more than seen it. I've done it.

TOMBI: You crap in the…?

MIZUKANE: Your sister's… *(Gestures with fist, 'shagging'.)* … the Red Demon.

TOMBI: What?!

MIZUKANE: And I mean that with all due respect.

TOMBI: *(To audience.)* That day, Mizukane seemed to have less upstairs than the left side of my own brain. I can tell you, jealousy makes the left side of the brain very stupid.

MIZUKANE: Tombi?

TOMBI: Yeah?

MIZUKANE: I want to tell you something.

TOMBI: Oh.

MIZUKANE: You remember a couple of months ago, when I made the breakthrough with Red Demon? We were up on the cliff and we saw that huge flock of gannets out at sea.

TOMBI: Gannets?

MIZUKANE: You pointed at them and went Oh God.

TOMBI: At gannets?

MIZUKANE: Yeah. And then Red Demon went Oh God too.

TOMBI: Oh yeah, when the Red Demon went, Oh God, I went running around shouting Oh God with him. It was excellent. Why was I saying that again?

MIZUKANE: Well, nothing to do with gannets *per se.*

TOMBI: Oh, I thought you said –

MIZUKANE: It had nothing to do with flocks of birds or signs of fish or anything like that. There was…something else.

TOMBI: Something else?

MIZUKANE: A ship, Tombi. You saw a faraway ship.

TOMBI: I did?

MIZUKANE: We all did. Glinting like silver in the sun. A ship…

TOMBI: A ship…

MIZUKANE: Yeah, but whose ship, Tombi? Who could have been steering that ship?

TOMBI: Who is it?

MIZUKANE: All I know is, since that day, an unbelievable amount of bottles have washed up. Stacks of them. And with no storm to bring them here neither.

TOMBI: Probably empties like always.

MIZUKANE: That's what I thought…till I checked inside them.

TOMBI: You checked inside them? What did you find?

MIZUKANE: Let's just say, a little bit more than the sound of the surf.

TOMBI: What? Messages you mean?!

MIZUKANE: You know the subtle surveillance I've been effecting on the Red Demon and your sister? Well, the day before yesterday, the meaning of what's inside those bottles began to take shape…

TOMBI: It did?

MIZUKANE: Like a silver ship appearing out of the haze…

TOMBI: Like the ship we saw?

MIZUKANE: Exactly like that, Tombi. And it scares the shit out of me.

TOMBI: But what's in the bottles? What do they say?

MIZUKANE: I don't know for sure. It's like the sun's in my eyes. But I feel it.

TOMBI: Oh Mizukane!

MIZUKANE: Now listen to me. If these messages are what I think they are, we have to be extremely careful. Your sister could be in serious danger. And the villagers… well. Who knows. And the Red Demon… *(Shrugs.)* So, not a word, yeah? *(With significance.)* Deceit is the morning sickness of the birth of truth.

TOMBI: What?

MIZUKANE: Keep schtum.

TOMBI: Right.

MIZUKANE: Keep what?

TOMBI: Schtum. I keep schtum about the bottles.

MIZUKANE: Spot on.

TOMBI: *(To audience.)* And because I am such a moron, there were very few people by the next morning who didn't know about the bottles and the messages that might be in them. Spot on, yes.

Beach.

MAN ONE: Hey, quick get that bottle…

MAN TWO: What, have I got a sign here says 'Mizukane' or something?

MAN ONE: Just check inside it, won't kill you.

MAN TWO: *(*Won't kill me*)*, it's empty, pal.

MAN THREE: Have a bloody look!

MAN TWO: All right, all right, keep your – *(He stops.)*

MAN THREE: What?

MAN TWO: ...dunno...

MAN THREE: Is it...?

MAN TWO: There's nothing here but...must be...

MAN ONE: What...demon language?

MAN THREE: *Red* Demon language....

MAN ONE: Oh God...

MAN TWO: Oh God...

Enter ELDER.

JUDGE: Bring the Red Demon and That Woman here immediately!

TOMBI: *(To audience.)* And then the cock crowed, and the dawn came, and the trial on the beach began. There's always someone who lives by a beach who's an expert at fishing out the truth...

SCENE 12

Court. JUDGE, THAT WOMAN, MIZUKANE and VILLAGERS take their positions.

JUDGE: This trial will be brief. I wish to hear only that which the court need hear. Now the accused stands before us today charged with treachery in the first degree. I need remind no-one of the consequences of such an act. However, I command those present to remain polite, courteous and above all, concise. No mucking about. Mizukane...

MIZUKANE: Yes, m'lord?

JUDGE: We see before us evidence of a great many bottles.

MIZUKANE: Yes, m'lord.

JUDGE: Divulge.

MIZUKANE: Yes, well, these are bottles found on the beach, m'lord. As you wisely suggest, there are a great many of them, sir.

JUDGE: Your point?

MIZUKANE: My point being that these bottles contain messages.

JUDGE: Messages?

MIZUKANE: Messages, your honour, which I believe have been directed personally to the accused.

THAT WOMAN: Oh what rubbish! He's talking utter –

JUDGE: Order!

THAT WOMAN: But your honour –

JUDGE: ORDER! I will tolerate no interruptions in this courtroom. You will have your chance. Mizukane, kindly proceed.

MIZUKANE: M'lord. It is my belief that the advent of the Red Demon has been no fluke.

JUDGE: A-ha.

MIZUAKNE. That in fact when it washed up on this shore, it was not so much by accident…as by design.

THAT WOMAN: Huh!

MIZUKANE: You see, when it saw its ship out there, on the waves – and Tombi can testify to this – it jumped for joy and started yelling Oh God. In other words, your honour m'lord, *it knew it was time for the signal.*

JUDGE: The what?!

THAT WOMAN: This is ludicrous!

JUDGE: Silence!

THAT WOMAN: This man is mad with jealousy, your honour! He'll do anything to shunt Hideki off this beach and get his mits on me! I mean, for God's sake, a signal?! How's Hideki supposed to send a signal? It's a joke!

MIZUKANE: Your honour, I am but a humble spokesperson. *Everyone's* picked up these bottles.

JUDGE: That Woman. Something constructive for you.

THAT WOMAN: Oh?

JUDGE: Command Red Demon to read to us all the message contained in Mizukane's bottle.

THAT WOMAN: Hideki? *(She points at bottle.)*

RED DEMON: I have a dream that one day freedom will ring from every hill and from every mountainside, every village and every hamlet, every state and every city…

JUDGE: Well. Rather revealing, wouldn't you say? That Woman, are you familiar with these words?

THAT WOMAN: I am.

VILLAGER ONE: And what do they mean?

THAT WOMAN: It's his dream.

VILLAGER ONE: Yes?

THAT WOMAN: I think the gist is 'Ring the bell quickly'.

VILLAGER TWO: Ah, the *bell.* Where?

THAT WOMAN: On every shore, as one, ring all the bells.

VILLAGER THREE: To what purpose?

THAT WOMAN: As his signal.

JUDGE: So we concur on the notion of a signal after all. I put it to you, That Woman, that this signal has less to do with some bizarre existential gesture, but rather more with the instigation of an invasion.

VILLAGERS: An invasion.

JUDGE: Let it be heard, of the most deadly intent!

THAT WOMAN: No, no, it's a signal of his *freedom!*

JUDGE: Claptrap.

THAT WOMAN: Look, he's making the whole thing up! How many times have I got to tell you? He's notorious! *(To RED DEMON.)* Tell them. Please. Your people aren't coming, are they? It's lies. There's no such thing as a ship or an invasion or anything is there?

RED DEMON: @@@.

THAT WOMAN: What?

VILLAGER TWO: What did it say?

THAT WOMAN: I don't understand, what do you mean?

RED DEMON: @@@@@@.

VILLAGER THREE: What is it saying woman!

THAT WOMAN: He's saying, he's saying…

RED DEMON: @@@@@.

THAT WOMAN: NO! He's saying, he's different! Oh god…

JUDGE: TELL US WHAT IT'S SAYING IMMEDIATELY!

THAT WOMAN: He…he wants to ring the bells, yes…to signal to his people on the ship…from every shore…the freedom…

RED DEMON: I have a dream…

THAT WOMAN: Shut up, shut up!

RED DEMON: Let freedom ring. Let freedom –

56

VILLAGER ONE: It confesses!

VILLAGER TWO: From the lips of the monster we hear the truth!

VILLAGER THREE: Demons are coming to devour us, one by one –

THAT WOMAN: He's not a monster or a demon! He's a person. People don't eat people. *He makes me feel more human than any of you!*

Shocked silence.

JUDGE: Which brings me rather nimbly to the secondary, related charge. Namely that…of 'contact'.

MIZUKANE: Hang on, what?

JUDGE: A point of contact has undoubtedly formed between That Woman and the Red Demon.

THAT WOMAN: Who could possibly…

JUDGE: Mizukane, have you not had occasion to witness evidence of 'contact' between That Woman and Red Demon in the time leading up to this trial?

MIZUKANE: Well, yeah, I mean….

JUDGE: And have you not borne witness to an emotional and physical bond growing between these two parties like vines in the dark?

MIZUKANE: Well I wouldn't put it quite like –

VILLAGER ONE: Answer the question.

MIZUKANE: Sure. But the the thing is –

JUDGE: The court must hear that the reason the Red Demon so closely resembles a human being in the eyes of That Woman is precisely because of this contact, this terrible, unholy…*proximity.*

VILLAGER TWO: So that means That Woman has become...

VILLAGER THREE: ...become a red demon too!

Court in uproar.

MIZUKANE: Whoh whoh whoh your honour. Hold up. The Red Demon, as you wisely observe, is a red demon. Can't fault it. But That Woman? She just got...entangled. Swept up in the frisson of events, like a mouse in a whirlpool.

JUDGE: Euphemisms, Mizukane? Not my bag of bananas!

MIZUKANE: No, m'lord, the truth. And the truth is that That Woman...is a victim. Yeah, of a most *ruthless* deceit.

JUDGE: That Woman is a traitor, conspirator and interloper of the first water.

MIZUKANE: Please, your honour, hear me out. She's not well. Her brother's a moron. She's been very vulnerable. Incredibly giving. *Too* giving, some might say.

JUDGE: Are you finished?

MIZUKANE: Fuku, tell the judge you'll have nothing more to do with Red Demon, yeah?

THAT WOMAN: He's not a demon.

MIZUKANE: Yeah, lovely, just tell the judge you don't know what the hell happened, you lost your mind and it's all been a total cock-up. Tell him.

THAT WOMAN: The judge?

MIZUKANE: What? Yes! Look, it doesn't matter what the demon *is.* Just tell the judge what you see. And that what you see, bold as brass, looking a little bit spooky, tiny bit kooky, is One Red Motherfucking Demon!

THAT WOMAN remains silent.

JUDGE: That Woman, I put it to you directly. What do you see before you in this courtroom today? Do you see a demon or do you see a human being?

THAT WOMAN: I see…myself.

Court goes beserk.

JUDGE: I hereby declare that both the accused are found guilty of treachery and all related offences. At daybreak tommorrow, the Red Demon and That Woman shall be brought onto this beach and executed by exposure to the rays of the sun. Any queries, I'm on the usual number. Take them to the cave!

SCENE 13

Sea Cave. THAT WOMAN and RED DEMON are held prisoner.

THAT WOMAN: Well, I think that went very well. Yes, I think that's what they call 'a bit of a result', no? I mean considering that nobody round here considered it particularly necessary to fill me in on the fact that an entire boatload of demons have been sitting out there for just the last six months waiting for the bell to invade… Couldn't have gone better.

Silence.

Are you. Deaf?

RED DEMON: @@@@@ …Uminomuko. [This is not the land beyond the sea.]

THAT WOMAN: What?

RED DEMON: @@@@@@ …Uminomuko.

THAT WOMAN: Is that 'beyond the sea' in your language?

RED DEMON: @@@@@@ …uminomuko… @@.

THAT WOMAN: These paintings…they are 'beyond the sea' aren't they?

RED DEMON: @@@@@@. [I don't know myself.]

THAT WOMAN: You don't know yourself? Then what are they? Why did you do them? And these letters. Carved. New. Why?

RED DEMON: @@@@@@@.

THAT WOMAN studies the wall.

THAT WOMAN: *(Reading.)* 'By the hand of Red Demon, resident of this cave… This painting is of my homeland. It represents beyond the sea. Yet I have never seen this land, for my people set sail long before I was born. We left a place where the average temperature is 138 degrees centigrade. We dwelt there in perfect bliss. But then, like coconuts drifting away from shore, we began our wandering. Many times we were washed up on a beach… but never the beach of our home. And we were never taken in or accepted, no matter where we landed. Only when I found myself on this beach did I genuinely believe that at last I was beyond the sea. My friends are offshore, waiting for me to ring a bell. The ringing will tell them that finally we have come home.'

RED DEMON: @@@@@@.

THAT WOMAN nods and moves to another wall.

@@@@@@@@@.

THAT WOMAN: *(Reading.)* 'Recently, bottles have been washing up with no messages in them. My friends have tired of waiting for a bell that will never sound. They have moved on.' *(To RED DEMON.)* Leaving you behind?

RED DEMON: @@@@@@.

THAT WOMAN: They probably think you're dead? But that's awful!

RED DEMON: @@@@@. [They're not awful.]

THAT WOMAN: Okay, they're not. But tomorrow you'll be dead as a dead thing, so. *(She shrugs and smiles.)* Still, I haven't lost hope. There's still time before sunrise. And even though we all know my brother… I guarantee he's stayed up all night and right this minute is devising a cunning plan to get us out of here.

SCENE 14

THAT WOMAN's house.

TOMBI: *(To audience.)* For some reason I slept like a log that night. Until, that is, I was awakened by a noise that sounded like something had stopped dead in my heart. After that, I couldn't get back to sleep. I lay listening to the sound of the waves folding over each other, and the layers of the sand falling and swishing. Then came a weeping noise. I thought it was just a sound coming off the nets. But thinking back…was it not Red Demon…all along?

Banging at the door.

Who is it?

MIZUKANE: It's me.

TOMBI: What's up?

MIZUKANE. Can't sleep.

TOMBI: Me too.

MIZUKANE: I can't handle it. The thought of your sister dying before I can shag the arse off her really depresses me.

TOMBI: Yes.

MIZUKANE: I'm such a tosser.

TOMBI: Yes.

MIZUKANE: That bloody court…it was obvious I was talking bollocks. Wasn't it? Except that sodding *demon* goes and tells everyone I'm bang on. Like I've rumbled him. I mean what are the odds on that?

TOMBI: Like the boy who runs around crying about the wolf.

MIZUKANE: Like, exactly. Precisely.

TOMBI: It's a toughie…

MIZUKANE: Like… *(He stops, then starts smiling.)* You daredevil…you little piece of magic…

TOMBI: What?

MIZUKANE: That's it…the boy who cried wolf!

TOMBI: What is he?

MIZUKANE: You and me Tombi, we're gonna run around this beach crying wolf.

TOMBI: We are?

MIZUKANE: Diversion tactics! I'll nick a boat, while you grab as much food as you can, meet me down the shore.

TOMBI: For my sister and the Red Demon?

MIZUKANE: In one.

TOMBI: You planning to get them away on a boat?

MIZUKANE: Don't be ridiculous, that'd just throw them together. We're going too.

TOMBI: Us too? The hero, the heroine and the heroine's moron brother…hmm, got a nice ring to it. Hold on, how does Red Demon fit in?

MIZUKANE: Navigator.

TOMBI: What? We're going to the land beyond the sea?

MIZUKANE: Red Demon's gonna take us just as far as his mates on that ship of his.

TOMBI: Oh. But, but…they might eat us…

MIZUKANE: No way. He'll owe us his life, for starters.

TOMBI: But what if they eat people they owe things to?

MIZUKANE: Well, if that happens, we'll have you on board.

TOMBI: Right.

MIZUKANE: Right.

TOMBI: So I'm going to be a wolf boy too?

MIZUKANE: Welcome to the firm.

SCENE 15

Beach. TOMBI and MIZUKANE rush around outside the cave yelling 'Wolf!' at the tops of their voices.

RED DEMON: @@@@@.

THAT WOMAN: Take it easy. There's only two people on the planet capable of this kinda crap.

TOMBI and MIZUKANE release them from the cave.

TOMBI: You okay?

THAT WOMAN: Fine, thanks.

TOMBI: Mizukane says he wants to shag the arse off you.

MIZUKANE: Tombi, how many times?

TOMBI: But you said there were only two kinds of women, those you wanna shag and those you –

MIZUKANE: Get moving.

TOMBI: Right.

THAT WOMAN: Wait a minute… *(They stop and look.)* …it's a calendar…with the days crossed off…

RED DEMON: @@@@@.

THAT WOMAN: Yeah, we have them as well.

RED DEMON: @@@@.

TOMBI: What'd he say?

THAT WOMAN: He's been crossing the days off since he got here…

TOMBI: Like we've been crossed for what we've done to him…

MIZUKANE: Come on, hurry up.

They move to the shore.

(Looking out to sea.) Just what the doctor ordered. A pea-souper. Right, let's shift. Untie that rope… *(TOMBI does so.)* …and they're off!

They push out the boat.

THAT WOMAN: Our mother went out to sea once, overcome with despair. It won't happen to me. I feel nothing but pride now that we can leave all this behind. I'm going to the land beyond the sea, the land our mother never reached.

They get in the boat.

RED DEMON quietly begins singing the song of his homeland. The others join in.

TOMBI: *(To audience.)* When the four of us set sail, we were filled with an overwhelming joy and excitement. We finally understood how the Von Trapp family must have felt when they sang Edelweiss fleeing from the Nazis over the Alps. However, the first of us to slip out of this feeling was Mizukane.

MIZUKANE: What the bloody hell are you on about?

THAT WOMAN and RED DEMON are giggling their heads off.

What do you mean it's gone? They're your mates! How can they have just…*left*?

RED DEMON: @@@@@.

THAT WOMAN: That's what I said!

RED DEMON: @@@@@@@.

Another fit of giggles. TOMBI joins in.

MIZUKANE: What are you laughing at, moron? *(Shakes his head.)* I should've seen this coming. Three days at sea, fuck all sign of a ship. *(Turns to RED DEMON.)* This bastard's stitched us up.

RED DEMON: @@@@@@.

MIZUKANE: What's it say?

THAT WOMAN: He said, 'I tricked the number one liar on the beach, so now I'm number one. From now on, you're number two.'

MIZUKANE: Comic wizadry.

RED DEMON: Best on the beach, second best on the beach, son of a beach!

More laughter from all except MIZUKANE.

MIZUKANE: Right, Tombi. We're going back.

THAT WOMAN: Back? Back where?

MIZUKANE: Where d'you think?

THAT WOMAN: You don't understand anything, do you? Take a look at that current, fisherman. *You haven't got a prayer.*

MIZUKANE: *(Looking.)* That's beautiful.

THAT WOMAN: We have to keep faith, we have to keep going…

MIZUKANE: Red Demon old son. Any revelations as to the actual locale of beyond the sea?

THAT WOMAN: @@@@@.

RED DEMON: Not a clue.

More laughter from RED DEMON and THAT WOMAN.

TOMBI: *(To audience.)* My sister and Red Demon never lost the good mood they were in. And I had never seen her like this, like a fish returned to the ocean. Like a mermaid…

Three-second blackout.

Lights up.

MIZUKANE: Not one, single sodding fish…

TOMBI: *(To audience.)* It was like they could smell our presence. All that came near us…was sharks.

MIZUKANE: Now that's what I call food. If we could catch one of them, oh boy…

RED DEMON: @@@@@@.

THAT WOMAN: There's a storm brewing.

RED DEMON: @@@@.

THAT WOMAN: That's why no fish.

MIZUKANE: Okay. Tombi, Plan B.

TOMBI: What?

MIZUKANE: Get out the grub you brought.

TOMBI: Oh, mm.

MIZUKANE: Pucker up ye taste buds and feel the – what's this?

TOMBI: It's for Red Demon.

MIZUKANE: It's all bloody flowers.

TOMBI: That's what he likes.

MIZUKANE: What? Well, where's ours?

TOMBI: Uhm, nowhere.

MIZUKANE: Eh?! I told you to get as much food as you could!

TOMBI: I did. One, two, a whole lot…

MIZUKANE: A whole – you fucking imbecile. What about us!

RED DEMON: *(Plucking a petal.)* @@@@?

MIZUKANE: Sorry?

RED DEMON: @@@@@. [Have a bite.]

MIZUKANE: You taking the piss? Here. How's this for a trick.

He throws all the flowers overboard.

OTHERS: NO!!

Three-second blackout.

Lights up.

THAT WOMAN: Aren't you a bit hungry?

TOMBI: I'm famished.

RED DEMON: I'm famished.

They burst out laughing again.

MIZUKANE: Shut the fuck up!

RED DEMON: He's angry because he's hungry.

TOMBI: *(To audience.)* When you get peckish, the gas makes your temper very short. But when you get famished, all you do is laugh your head off. Laughing just made us hungrier. And the hungrier we got, the more we cracked up. Total joy became our constant state.

Three-second blackout.

Lights up. RED DEMON and THAT WOMAN are lying down.

RED DEMON: @@@@.

He dies. Over the following dialogue, he steps from the boat and withdraws like a spirit, to the rhythm of the waves. The others refer to the space left behind, as if he were still present.

THAT WOMAN: Tombi, Hideki wants you to look out there for a second.

TOMBI: What is it?

THAT WOMAN: He thinks he just caught sight of the land beyond the sea.

TOMBI: Really?

He looks out.

THAT WOMAN: Can you see it?

TOMBI: No…no I can't. *(He looks at RED DEMON's space.)* Uh oh. Red Demon's not breathing.

They burst out laughing again.

(To audience.) Only the storm could take the breath from my laughing. As it came closer, the sea and the sky looked full of foreboding. The only ray of good cheer came from my little sister. Her brightness shone like the blue sky which would hang above her funeral…

Sound of a fierce storm.

SCENE 16

Beach. The storm rages. Three figures are washed up. VILLAGERS enter and find them lying on the sand, in an exact replica of Scene 1.

MAN ONE: They're still breathing.

MAN TWO: Pull 'em up quick.

MAN ONE: We gotta keep 'em warm.

WOMAN ONE: Any more of 'em?

WOMAN TWO: Doesn't look like it.

MAN ONE: Christ…it's *them*…

MAN TWO: They made it back…

WOMAN TWO: Look! That Woman's here too!

MAN ONE: That Woman?

WOMAN ONE: Sling her back in the sea. She's not bleedin' worth it.

MAN TWO: What d'you think you're doing? She's *alive*.

WOMAN TWO: Just leave her where she is, will you!

HAG's shack. HAG brings THAT WOMAN a bowl of soup.

THAT WOMAN: Thank you. It tastes so good.

HAG: That's shark's fin soup. Special. We thought we'd lost you to the waterfall at the end of the sea.

THAT WOMAN: What was that?

HAG: Aye. Thought you'd sailed right off the edge of the ocean and –

THAT WOMAN: No, I mean the soup. What did you say it was?

HAG: Oh, shark's fin. The fin of the shark…

THAT WOMAN: This isn't what shark's fin tastes like.

HAG: What, you've had it before, have you?

THAT WOMAN: Of course I have. Every day out at sea. This isn't it. I'm telling you, this isn't shark's fin at all!

She backs away.

MIZUKANE: What's all that about?

TOMBI: She's chucking up.

MIZUKANE: Chucking up?

TOMBI: Not a lot is coming out though.

MIZUKANE: Ah, she probably ate too quick after all this
time.

TOMBI: Yeah.

MIZUKANE: Wouldn't touch a thing out there, eh?

TOMBI: No.

They realise THAT WOMAN is staring at them.

Both turn slowly.

THAT WOMAN: *(Slowly.)* Did you say… 'shark's fin'?

MIZUKANE: *(Beat.)* How are you feeling?

THAT WOMAN: You said 'shark's fin', no?

MIZUKANE: You all right?

THAT WOMAN: I was in a daze. You gave me soup…

MIZUKANE: Tombi…

THAT WOMAN: And you said it was shark's fin, didn't you?
DIDN'T YOU?!

MIZUKANE: Did I?

THAT WOMAN: Yes you did godammit! What you gave me
wasn't shark's fin at all!

MIZUKANE: Please. You knew the score.

THAT WOMAN: I *what?*

MIZUKANE: You knew that wasn't shark's fin. After all, who
told you that it was?

THAT WOMAN: Are you insane?

MIZUKANE: You've never believed a word I've ever said. So
why believe then?

THAT WOMAN: Tombi –

MIZUKANE: Why?

THAT WOMAN: I need to hear it from my brother –

MIZUKANE: I thought I could keep you alive. I *wanted* to keep you alive. Because I love you. No, tell a lie. Because I want to make love to you. If you die, you'll be no bloody use to me.

THAT WOMAN: Tombi, please, tell me the truth. When I was out there, had Hideki already stopped breathing?

TOMBI: Huh?

THAT WOMAN: Or was he was still breathing, faintly?

TOMBI: I don't follow, Sis.

THAT WOMAN: No, you do follow. Was Hideki dead by the time I ate the shark's fin soup?

MIZUKANE: Why bother that pretty little head, eh? You were dying. Don't you get it? There was Nothing To Eat. Christ, you were so weak, I was terrified soon you wouldn't be able to keep down anything at all. And then…I saw it's body, right there, right under our noses. Whatever you think, it wasn't a demon or a human by then. It was just a thing. A hunk of meat. It was *food.*

THAT WOMAN: So you ate him.

MIZUKANE: I ate it.

THAT WOMAN: And you too Tombi?

TOMBI: Me too. It was delicious.

THAT WOMAN: And what about me?

TOMBI: What?

THAT WOMAN: Did his flesh go in my mouth?

TOMBI: Even though you were laughing and laughing…no. We couldn't make you eat.

MIZUKANE: So I took it upon myself, lying bastard that I am, to tell you a little porky pie. 'Don't worry,' I said. 'This is shark's meat. The fin of the shark. Eat it,' I said. 'And live.'

THAT WOMAN: When I met him for the first time, I said to him 'You're a demon. And you're a demon because you eat humans.' I was wrong. Demons don't eat humans. Humans eat demons. They eat them to survive. *(Beat.)* I remember: You held out your hand, in front of those people, and you said: 'Eat it and live.' So I ate. And I lived.

TOMBI: *(To audience.)* My little sister died two days later. She threw herself from the tallest cliff high above the beach. From that day, Mizukane was left without a soul. As for me, I'm basically the same as ever. I survive by not knowing very much about anything. Sometimes though, I see Red Demon and my sister laughing their heads off on that boat. My sister was laughing, but I reckon she was without hope then. I too laugh when I picture her like that. It helps me understand what it means to live without hope. I won't lose my hope though. Because things continue to wash up. When I breathe in, what is beyond the sea comes to this shore. When I breathe out, it leaves again, back out to sea. I am breathing in concert with the land beyond the sea. And beyond the sea, at the very bottom, lies my little sister's heart.

Lights fade.

Blackout.

Printed in the USA
CPSIA information can be obtained
at www.ICGtesting.com
LVHW021000171024
794056LV00004B/1260